Discover
PLANETS

cupcake

This edition first published in 2010
by Alligator Books Ltd.
Cupcake is an imprint of
Alligator Books Ltd.,
Gadd House, Arcadia Avenue,
London N3 2JU

Printed in China

Illustrator: David Cornish
Author: Adele F. Stephens

Contents

The School Trip to Space!   4

The Solar System   5

How Big is the Solar System?   6

The Planets   7

The Sun and Gravity   8

Mercury and Venus   8

Earth   10

Mars   11

Jupiter   12

Saturn, Uranus and Neptune   13

The Night Sky   14

The Stars   15

The Moon   16

Can We Live on the Moon?   17

Shining 3D Star   18

Solar System Mobile   19

3D Model of the Moon   20

Construct a Space Shuttle   21

Solar Power Experiment   22

Create a Sundial   23

Exploding Volcano   24

Make a Comet   25

Craft an Alien Spaceship   26

Make Your Own Milky Way   27

Glossary   28

Index   30

The School Trip to Space!

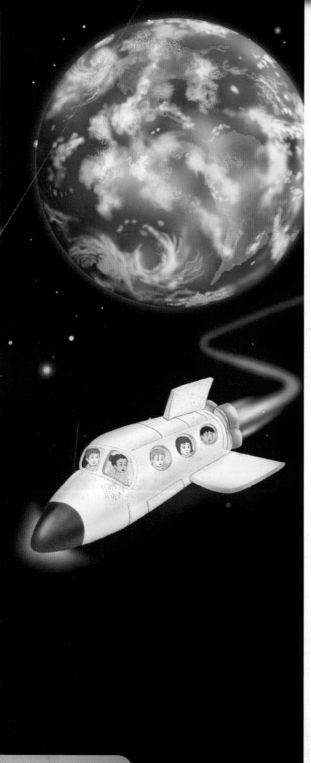

Tom, Sally, Beth, Rosie and Joe are excited because their school trip is today! They climb aboard the spaceship and prepare for take off – they are going on a trip to Space! The spaceship's computer has a giant screen that flashes information when the students ask questions. As they settle into their seats, they learn that they live on a small, rocky planet called Earth.

> **Earth orbits, or travels around, a big star called the Sun. With them are a family of 8 planets, over 60 moons, billions of icy comets, millions of rocky asteroids, some minor planets and lots of dust and gas.**
>
> **All together, this is called the Solar System.**

"Didn't Pluto get downgraded?" asked Sally.
"Yes, scientists now know that Pluto is a large asteroid, not a planet," replied Joe.

> **Each planet spins on its own axis, which is an imaginary straight line. They zip around and around like a spinning top as they orbit the sun. One full spin is a planet's day and night. Some spin very fast, while others move at a cosmic snail's pace.**

Did you know?

One year, or 365 Earth days, is how long it takes the Earth to travel once around the Sun.

The Solar System

The spaceship shook and roared as its e[...]
Beth. "We're ready for lift off in T minus 5, 4,

The children stared in wonder at the
enormous expanse of Space as their
galactic voyager began to dip and weave
across the Milky Way.

"Don't look directly at the Sun; it'll hurt
your eyes," said Rosie.
"Where is the
Sun?" asked Joe.

The Sun is in the middle of the Solar
System, but if you look up on a clear
night you can see millions of other stars
twinkling in the sky.
Our Sun is one of more than one
hundred billion stars in a huge group, or
galaxy of stars called the Milky Way.

Big is the Solar System?

Sizes and distances in space are so colossal it can be difficult to imagine them. To help you understand, think about how big planet Earth is.
Now look at the planets below that have been arranged from largest to smallest. Look how tiny Earth is compared to the Sun!

Jupiter

Saturn

Uranus

Neptune

Earth

Venus

Mars

Mercury

The Planets

"I know a really fun trick to remember the order of the planets," said Beth. "It's simple, take the first letter of each planet and make a word."

Did you know?

The sunlight we see today started out in the heart of the Sun 30,000 years ago. It took most of this time for the sunlight to leave the Sun's core, then just 8 minutes to reach Earth after this!

Mercury →

Venus →

Earth →

Mars →

Jupiter →

Saturn →

Uranus →

Neptune →

Can you make up your own fun sentence? Like this one:
My Very Elegant Mum Just Served Us Nibbles.

FACTOID
EVERY OBJECT IN THE SOLAR SYSTEM REVOLVES AROUND THE SUN.

Computer, this is amazing," said Tom, while gazing from the spaceship's window, "but how did the Solar System get here?"

It came from a giant cloud of gas and dust called the Solar Nebula. When it collapsed, under the weight of its own gravity, the middle of this spinning cloud formed a tiny star. This star grew and became the Sun.

"Why don't planets just float off into space?" asked Sally.
"Gravity," said Joe, reading his notes. "Gravity pulls objects towards one another."

Yes, the Sun's gravitational force keeps them together. Sol, our Sun, is about 4.8 billion years old. Invisible particles stream from the Sun and make up what is called Solar Wind. When these specks pass the North and South Poles of Earth, they shimmer spectacularly like ribbons of light in our sky.

"The particles that we see shimmering are incredible; they are called the Aurora Borealis or the Northern Lights," said Tom.
"I saw them in Norway."

Did you know?

The Sun's brightness is equal to 4 trillion 100 watt light bulbs!

Mercury and Venus

"Hey, that little planet looks just like our Moon!" exclaimed Beth, as the spaceship approached the planet Mercury.

"Mercury has hardly any atmosphere. There's nothing to stop meteors or comets from crashing onto its surface; that's why it has craters like the Moon," said Joe, reading his notes.

Known as a dead planet, Mercury has little air, no water and is very dry and hot. At night temperatures can plunge to hundreds of degrees below freezing! Mercury's moonless sky is black at night.

Did you know?
Mercury is the speediest of all the planets, orbiting at abound 30 miles (48 kilometers) per second!

"I read in science class that during the day, solar rays can be seven times as hot on Venus as they are on Earth, reaching a scorching 840° F (450° C)," said Rosie. "Computer, which planet in the Solar System is the hottest?"

That's Venus. Although its atmosphere is unlike ours now, many scientists think Venus may have once been a tropical paradise. With its mountains, volcanoes, and canyons, it could have had lots of water and may have even been inhabited!

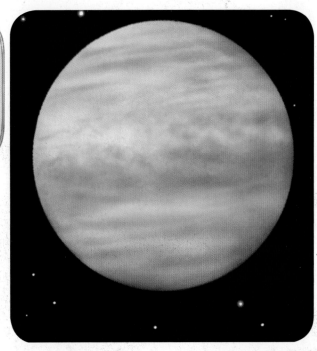

FACTOiD
VENUS IS THE BRIGHTEST OBJECT SEEN FROM THE EARTH AT NIGHT.

Earth

"I recognise that blue planet," said Sally. "And it is the 3rd rock from the Sun," added Beth.

"It's the Earth!" yelled the children.

"Approximately 75 percent of Earth is covered with water, which is why it looks so blue from Space," said Joe looking at his book again.

Earth has existed for about 4 ½ billion years. We live on the only planet with an atmosphere that allows for the perfect temperature and that has water in liquid form. Life on Earth is possible because it's just the right distance from the Sun.

Mars

"My book says that Mars is known as the Red Planet because of its red soil," said Joe.

Mars has just two moons, which isn't many compared to Jupiter, which has about 63 moons. Mars has violent dust, wind and sandstorms. This planet has the largest volcano in the Solar System, called Olympus Mons. It's bigger than the whole of the Great Britain!

Did you know?

Meteorites are tiny pieces of rock. In space they're called meteoroids but on Earth they're known as meteors or shooting stars.

Jupiter

"Look, it's Jupiter," said Rosie as the spaceship's engines roared, "it would take us forever to travel around that monster-sized planet! Did you know it's made of gas and has no solid surface at all?"

"Computer, is Jupiter the biggest planet in the Solar System?" asked Sally.

Yes, it weighs more than all of the other planets put together!
The first of four gas planets, this giant takes almost 12 years to orbit the Sun. It's known for its Great Red Spot, which is actually a huge storm that has been raging on the planet for hundreds of years.

FACTOID
BETWEEN MARS AND JUPITER, THERE ARE LUMPS OF METAL AND ROCK CALLED ASTEROIDS THAT FLY AROUND. THIS IS KNOWN AS THE ASTEROID BELT.

Saturn, Uranus and Neptune

"We've flown around some totally amazing planets," said Rosie. "Which are we passing next?"
"The remaining three planets that are made of gas – Saturn, Uranus and Neptune," answered Beth.

"Computer, do you have any more interesting facts?" asked Sally.

Uranus is the coldest planet in the Solar System. It doesn't spin, but rolls like a football, which means that each day and night lasts for 42 years!

Neptune, the smallest and last of the gas planets, has wild storms with winds of 1,250 miles (2,000 kilometres) per hour!

Uranus and Neptune appear blue in colour. This is because of the methane gas that freezes into a cloud above their outer layer of hydrogen gas.

Saturn is the only planet that is less dense than water. If you dropped Saturn into a giant bathtub, it would float!

"I can see Saturn, I recognise its seven beautiful rings, which are made up of ice, dust and rock. Some pieces are as small as dust, other chunks are as big as a bus and others the size of buildings! The rings look solid but they aren't," said Tom.

The Night Sky

"Just look at all the beautiful patterns the stars make. If I connect the dots, I see shapes," said Beth.

"The patterns are called constellations," said Sally.

"Why can't we see constellations during the day?" asked Tom.

"I know the answer," replied Sally, "the sun's light is too dazzling to see starlight in the daytime."

FACTOID
OUR OCEAN'S TIDES ARE CREATED BY THE MOON, WHOSE GRAVITY PULLS THE WATER.

More than 10,000 years ago, our ancestors were drawing pictures of the stars they saw above them.
A constellation is a group of stars that form patterns and twinkle in our night sky. Many were named after animals and characters from myths.

The ancient Greeks named the constellations after their heroes and gods.

The children's spaceship zigzagged across space as they gazed at the stars. "But how did they all get here? Do stars live forever?" asked Rosie.

The Stars

"Eventually a star will die when its gases have run out, but this can take a really long time," said Joe reading from his notebook.

A star begins as a twirling cloud of gas and particles of dust called a Nebula. These particles clump together and then collapse inward making a core and a star is born. As the star heats up, its gases explode and it twinkles.

Did you know?

Stonehenge was built in England 5,000 years ago. Some people believe it was used as an observatory to view the stars.

FACTOID
SOME STARS COLLAPSE CREATING A DENSE AND INVISIBLE BALL CALLED A BLACK HOLE.

The Moon

"Computer, is it true that the Moon has no air and no climate?" asked Tom.

Yes, and that is why footprints left by astronauts on the Moon's surface will never blow away! Our moon, Lunar, doesn't have any light of its own. We can see it so clearly because of the Sun's reflection bouncing off of it.

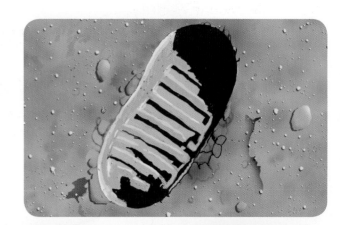

Did you know?

It would take 142 days to get to the moon if you were travelling at 70 mph (113 kph)!

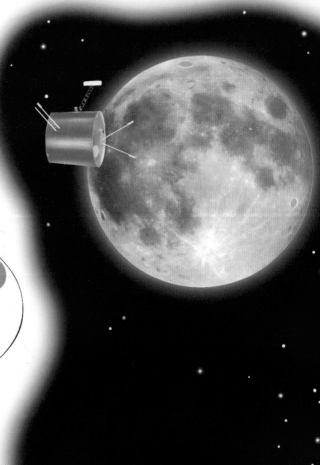

Can We Live on the Moon?

"Computer, can we visit other planets?" asked Rosie, "or take a holiday on the Moon?"

> **Scientists find exciting new things all the time but, right now, the Moon and all of the other planets simply don't have the right atmosphere, temperature or water supply for us to be able to visit or live on them.**

"How do astronauts and scientists explore our Universe?" asked Tom.

> **Scientists can use very powerful telescopes to view or to take pictures of the Solar System from Earth. There are also space shuttles that carry astronauts on special fact-finding missions. Space probes, which are unmanned spacecrafts, can explore places where it's too dangerous for astronauts to visit.**

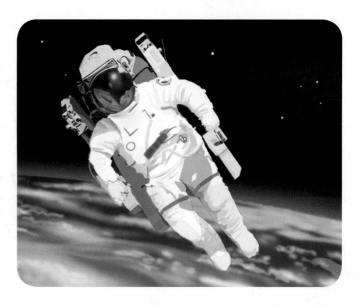

"It looks like we're heading back to Earth now," said Beth.
"This has been a great trip," said Joe, "and every time I look up at the stars in the sky, I'll think of how amazing our Universe truly is."

SHINING 3D STAR

You will need:

- Stiff paper or cardboard
- Crayons or markers (optional)
- Scissors
- Glue and string
- Silver and gold or white glitter
- Glow-in-the-dark paint (optional)

How to make it:

1. Draw 2 identical stars onto the cardboard as shown.

2. Carefully cut them out.

3. You can colour in or draw patterns (optional).

4. Cover your stars in a thin layer of glue and sprinkle on the glitter. You can use a different colour paint for each star. Art shops sell glow-in-the-dark paint that can be used for a real-life effect! Shake off any excess glitter.

5. Make a slit in the top point of one star and at the bottom centre of the other.

6. Slot the two stars together using these slits.

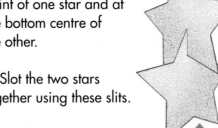

7. Make a small hole in the top and thread some string through the hole to hang your star and watch it sparkle!

SOLAR SYSTEM

Make your very own simple but amazing Solar System mobile right here on Earth!

You will need:

- The 8 planets from your box
- Yellow paint or markers
- Eight lengths of nylon string from your box
- Cardboard
- Scissors
- Gold glitter (optional)
- Glue

How to make it:

1. Push a length of thread through the hole in each planet then tie with a loop.

2. For the top of the mobile, cut out a circle from the cardboard, about 10 in. (25 cm) in diameter. Colour it in. Next, make a Sun to hang underneath the top, in the centre of your planets. The Sun circle should be approximately 4 in. (10 cm) in diameter. Colour this yellow and add glitter (optional).

3. Make 8 holes around the rim and one in the centre of the large circle.

4. Push one planet's thread through each hole. Secure.

5. Hang the Sun in the centre of the large circle.

6. Now, hang the eight planets around the rim of the large circle.

7. To hang your mobile, make 3 or more holes (equally spaced) in the circle and thread and tie the remaining string as shown. Hang it somewhere suitable and watch your planets spin.

3D MODEL OF THE MOON

Make a really fun papier-mache 3D model of the moon. Papier-mache can be messy so wear an apron or an old shirt.

You will need:

- One balloon
- Lots of newspaper
- Flour and water for the glue
- Pot and spoon to stir the glue
- Paint brushes and poster paint
- Cardboard for the base

How to make it:

1. Blow up the balloon and tie it carefully.

2. Boil 1200ml of water in a pot.

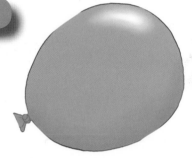

3. In a bowl, mix 30g of flour with a cup of cold water. Mix to a smooth consistency. When free of lumps, add the mixture to the water in the pot. Gently boil, stirring constantly for two or three minutes until the mixture thickens. Leave to cool before you use.

4. Tear up lots of long, 1 inch (2.5cm) wide strips from the newspaper.

5. Cut out a large rectangle from the cardboard for the moon to sit on.

6. Dip the strips of paper into the floury glue, wiping off any excess.

7. Wrap lots of layers around the balloon and the rectangle base. Leave overnight to dry (this may take longer). Pop the balloon and there you have your moon!

8. Colour the base black like Space. Paint your dry moon with poster paint, then use household glue to stick the moon to its base. Now you can display your moon for everyone to see!

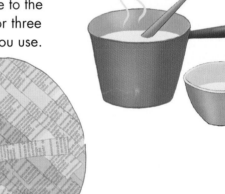

CONSTRUCT A SPACE SHUTTLE

NASA's space orbiters are called Discover, Atlantis, and Endeavor. They travel into space and allow scientists to study, learn and discover amazing things about our universe. Craft your own space shuttle and make your own designs!

You will need:

- A kitchen towel tube
- White cardboard and white paper
- Red tissue paper
- Black tissue paper
- Scissors
- Markers
- Glue

How to make it:

1. Using the white paper, cover the kitchen towel tube and glue into place.

2. Place some glue inside both ends of the kitchen towel tube.

3. Crumple the black tissue paper, enough to sit inside one glue-filled end and make sure it sticks out slightly (this is the front of the shuttle).

4. Cut the red tissue paper into 2 in. (5 cm) long ribbons and attach inside the other glued end.

5. Take the cardboard and carefully cut out a triangle and glue it to the paper towel roll.

6. Use your markers to colour in your space shuttle with your own designs or write NASA on the side.

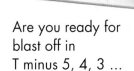

Are you ready for blast off in T minus 5, 4, 3 …

SOLAR POWER EXPERIMENT

Harness the power of the Earth's nearest star, the Sun, to make a solar-style sweet treat!

You will need:

- Four plain biscuits
- Eight mini marshmallows
- Two small milk chocolate bars
- One 8 x 11 in. (approx. 20 x 28 cm) glass baking dish
- A thermometer to measure outside air temperature (optional)
- Aluminium foil to cover the baking dish
- Hot, sunny weather

How to make it:

1. Place 2 biscuits in the bottom of the glass dish with a chocolate bar on top.

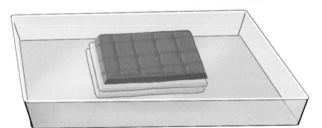

2. Put 8 mini marshmallows on top of the other crackers and cover with aluminium foil.

3. Place the pan in full sunlight in really warm weather (away from insects and animals).

4. Leave the dish outside until the heat of the sun melts the chocolate and marshmallows.

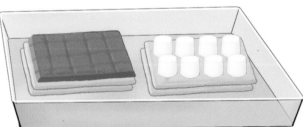

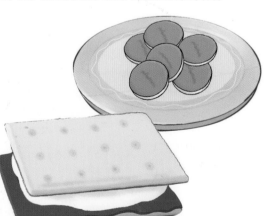

5. Put one chocolate covered biscuit and one marshmallow covered biscuit together and enjoy your solar-styled treat!

CREATE A SUNDIAL

For many centuries people didn't have clocks, so they could only tell time by watching the shadows of the sun. Leave your watch off for a day and tell the time with a sundial!

You will need:

- A large paper cup with a plastic lid and a straw
- A watch
- A pen and a pencil
- Sticky tape
- Some sand or pebbles to weigh down the cup
- A compass
- A very sunny day – two days would be perfect

How to make it:

1. Poke a hole in the side of the cup 2 in. (5 cm) from the top, with your pencil. Push the straw through and fill the cup half way with sand or pebbles.

2. Fasten the lid securely and push the straw through the holes on the lid and the side.

3. The straw should stick out of the top by 2 in. (5 cm). Tape the other end of the straw to the side. This will be your sundial.

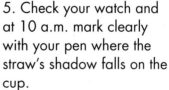

4. Place the sundial on a flat surface. Then, use a compass (the red finger points North) to point the straw to the North.

5. Check your watch and at 10 a.m. mark clearly with your pen where the straw's shadow falls on the cup.

6. Repeat every hour until around 3 p.m.

7. The next day, use the shadow of the straw to try telling the time. Check against your watch – is it right?

EXPLODING VOLCANO

Three times higher than Mount Everest, the volcano Olympus Mons on Mars is the biggest volcano in the Solar System. Make your very own exploding volcano with household items!

You will need:

- Two tablespoons of baking soda
- 720g of flour
- 475ml warm water
- 580g table salt
- Four tablespoons cooking oil
- Plastic drinks bottle and a baking tray
- Dishwasher detergent
- Food colouring and vinegar

How to make it:

1. Mix the water, salt, cooking oil and flour until the mixture is smooth and firm.

2. Stand the plastic bottle in the baking tray and mould the dough around it into a volcano shape. Don't cover the hole or get dough inside of it.

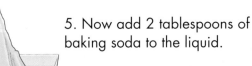

3. Fill the bottle almost to the top with warm water and a drop of red food colouring.

4. Add 6 drops of detergent into the bottle.

5. Now add 2 tablespoons of baking soda to the liquid.

6. Very slowly, pour vinegar into the bottle.

7. Watch out, eruption time!

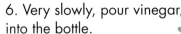

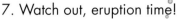

MAKE A COMET

Comets are dusty, little space balls that are made up of ice and rock. When they head toward the sun, their tails are behind them and when they whizz away their tails take the lead! Make your own comet – you could even make two!

You will need:

- A styrofoam ball (a tennis ball would work just as well)
- Scissors
- Glue
- Sticky tape
- Aluminium foil
- A pencil

How to make it:

1. Cut the ribbon into equal lengths; then tie together at one end and knot.

2. Make a hole in the styrofoam ball with your pencil and fill it with glue.

3. Push the knotted end of the ribbons into your pencil-made hole.

4. If using a tennis ball, secure the ribbons with tape.

5. Cut a piece of foil about 7 in. x 7 in. (18 cm x 18 cm) and cover your ball.

6. Make sure your comet's tail is coming through the foil.

7. In a safe space, throw your comet to make it fly!

CRAFT AN ALIEN SPACESHIP

Craft an alien spaceship of your very own!

You will need:

- A paper bowl
- Two large paper plates
- Scissors
- Double-sided sticky tape
- Glow-in-the-dark or regular stickers (optional)
- Coloured markers

How to make it:

1. With your scissors, carefully make two cuts in the bowl, about 2 in. (5 cm) apart, as shown.

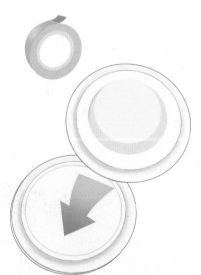

2. Take a length of the double-sided tape.

3. Stick the two plates together using the tape; one should be inside the other.

4. Tape the rim of your bowl to the bottom of the plates.

5. Decorate it with stickers (optional).

6. Colour your spaceship and draw any design you like.

7. Toss your spaceship and watch it take off!

TIP If you double up the plates, your spaceship will fly better.

MAKE YOUR OWN MILKY WAY

Our planet lies in one of the arms of a large spiral galaxy called the Milky Way. Make your own Milky Way and see it shine!

You will need:

- Thick black paper
- A white crayon
- Glue
- White or silver glitter (other colours optional)
- Old newspapers

How to make it:

1. The Milky Way, our spiral galaxy, has 5 arms and a circular centre.

2. Place old newspapers on a flat surface.

3. Using your white crayon, draw a sketch of the Milky Way on the black paper.

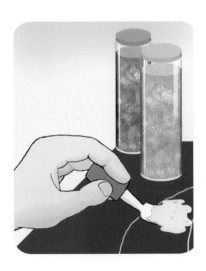

4. Take the glue and trace the drawing.

5. Sprinkle glitter onto the glue.

6. Tilt the paper to shake off any excess glitter.

7. Hang up your Milky Way and watch it shine!

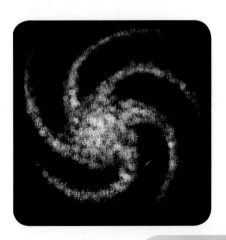

Glossary

Asteroids: rocky objects that can measure a few hundred miles/kilometres across. They fly around the asteroid belt, which is between Jupiter and Mars.

Astronomer: a scientist who studies Space.

Astronaut: someone who travels in Space.

Atmosphere: a layer of gas around a planet, like the air on Earth. The thickest part of the Earth's atmosphere is from the surface to approximately 9 miles/15 kilometres high.

Black Hole: the centre of a star that has collapsed. The gravity is so strong that it sucks in everything nearby.

Comet: dusty space balls made of ice and rock in orbit around the Sun.

Constellation: groups of stars that you can see from Earth that make different patterns in the sky. There are 88 recognised constellations.

Crater: a hole on the moon or on the surface of a planet.

Galaxy: a group of millions or billions of stars, gas, dust and planets held together by gravity.

Gravity: the natural force that pulls objects towards one another.

Light Year: the distance travelled by light in one year. One light year is approximately 5,900,000,000,000 miles /9,500,000,000,000 kilometres.

Meteors: a small piece of extraterrestrial matter that becomes visible as a shooting star or falling star when it enters the Earth's atmosphere. While still outside the atmosphere, it is called a meteoroid.

Meteorite: a stony or metallic mass of matter that has fallen to the Earth's surface from outer space.

Milky Way: the name of our Galaxy, which contains the Solar System.

Nebula: a cloud of gas and dust

Orbit: the path of an object when it travels around another object, like how the planets orbit the Sun.

Revolution: the movement of a planet in orbit around the Sun.

Rotation: the spin of a planet or star on its axis.

Satellite: an object that orbits a planet. The Earth has man-made satellites which we have launched into space, it also has one natural satellite which is the Moon.

Solar System: the Sun, 8 planets including Earth, over 60 moons, billions of icy comets, millions of rocky asteroids, some minor planets and lots of dust and gas.

Solar Wind: a steady flow of particles that stream out from the Sun.

Star: an object, like the Sun, that contains gases which heat it and make it twinkle, some are easy to see from Earth at night.

Supernova: the explosion of a star that becomes very luminous in the process.

Index

A
Asteroids 4, 12
Atmosphere 9, 10
Aurora Borealis 8
Astronauts 16, 17

B
Black Hole 15

C
Comet 4, 7
Constellations 14

E
Earth 4, 6, 7, 8, 10, 17

G
Galaxy 28
Gravity 8, 14
Gas Planets 12, 13

J
Jupiter 6, 7, 12

L
Light Year 28

M
Mars 6, 7, 11
Mercury 6, 7, 9
Meteorites 9, 11
Moons 5, 11
Moon (Earth's) 9, 16
Milky Way 5

N
Neptune 6, 7, 13
Nebula 15
Northern Lights 8

O
Olympus Mons volcano 11

S
Saturn 6, 7, 13
Shooting Stars 11
Solar System 5, 9, 11, 12
Solar Wind 29
Solar Nebula 8
Stars 4, 5, 8, 14, 15
Sun 4, 5, 6, 7, 8, 10, 14
Stonehenge 15

T
Trick to remember
the planets 7

U
Uranus 6, 7, 13

V
Venus 6, 7, 9

Northern Hemisphere

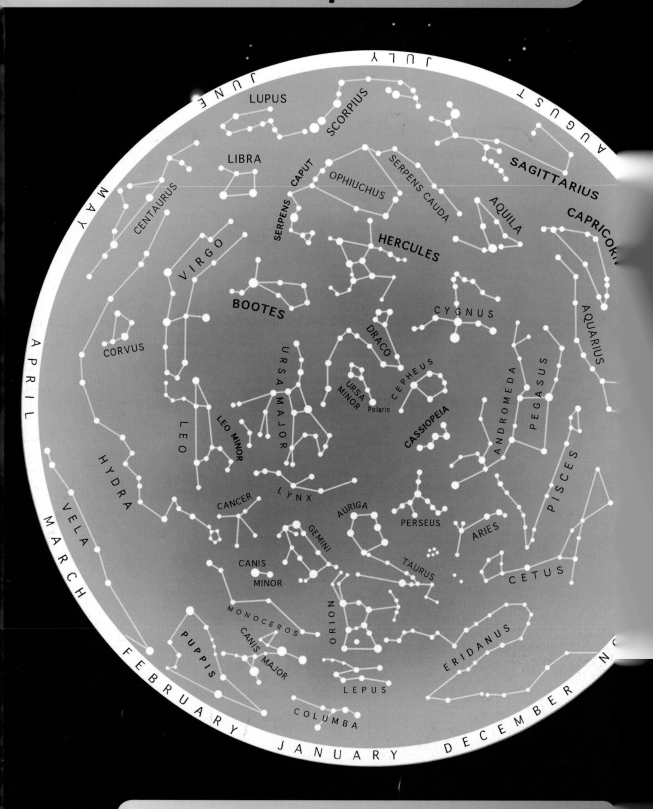

To use the maps, first find the current month, then turn the
map around until the current month is at the bottom. If
you are looking at the Northern Hemisphere sky, then face
South at night.

To use the maps, first find the current month, then turn the map around until the current month is at the bottom. If you are looking at the Southern Hemisphere sky, then face North at night.

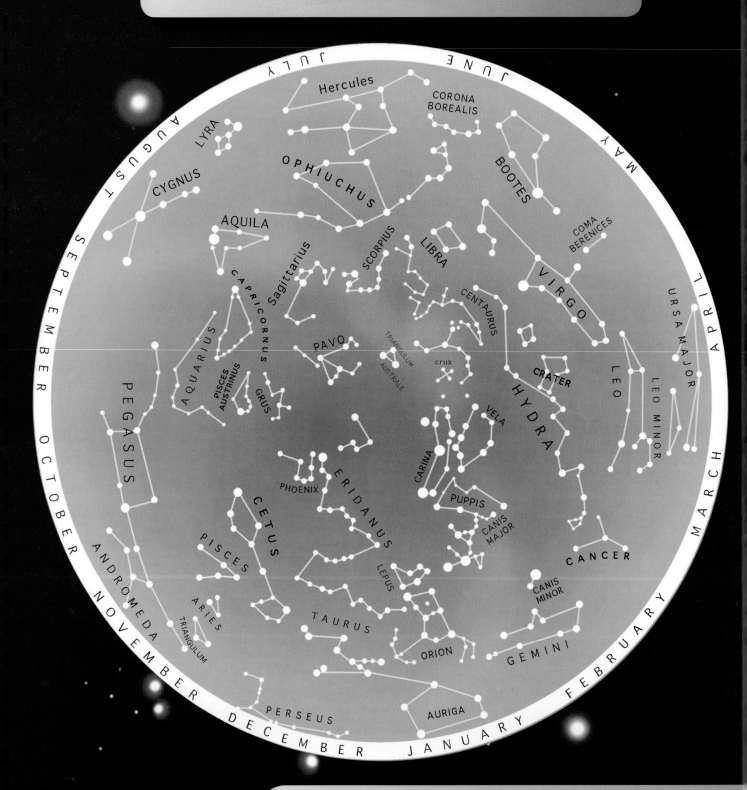

Southern Hemisphere